NATURE'S ULTIMATE DISASTERS

TOP 10 WORST

TSUNAMIS

Louise and Richard Spilsbury

PowerKiDS
press
New York

Published in 2017 by
The Rosen Publishing Group, Inc.
29 East 21st Street, New York, NY 10010

Cataloging-in-Publication Data

Names: Spilsbury, Louise.
Title: Top 10 worst tsunamis / Louise and Richard Spilsbury.
Description: New York : PowerKids Press, 2017. | Series: Nature's ultimate disasters | Includes index.
Identifiers: ISBN 9781499430813 (pbk.) | ISBN 9781499430837 (library bound) | ISBN 9781499430820 (6 pack)
Subjects: LCSH: Tsunamis--Juvenile literature. | Tsunami damage--Juvenile literature.
Classification: LCC GC221.5 S65 2017 | DDC 363.34'94--dc23

Produced for Rosen by Calcium
Editors for Calcium Creative Ltd: Sarah Eason and Harriet McGregor
Designers: Paul Myerscough and Simon Borrough
Picture research: Rachel Blount

Picture credits: Cover: Shutterstock: M Taira; Inside: NOAA/National Geophysical Data Center: Cpl. Megan Angel, U.S. Marine Corps 25, Hugh Davies. University of PNG 17, Katherine Mueller, IFRC 1, Harry Yeh, University of Washington 9l, 9r; Shutterstock: 3777190317 27, Anton Balazh 19, Steven Collins 4–5, Johan W. Elzenga 6–7, Everett Historical 13, Nickolay Stanev 21, Wickerwood 7; USGS: 11, 23; Wikimedia Commons: Nesnad/The Osaka Mainichi 15.

Manufactured in the United States of America

CPSIA Compliance Information: Batch #BW17PK: For Further Information contact Rosen Publishing, New York, New York at 1-800-237-9932.

Contents

TSUNAMI DANGER

Tsunamis are huge and destructive ocean waves that can cause terrible natural disasters. When a tsunami hits land, it is like a high and fast-moving wall of water. It can destroy or wash away everything in its path.

This valley in Thailand was completely engulfed during a tsunami.

How Dangerous?

Smaller tsunamis may wash onto a coastline like a quickly rising **tide**. They might only gently flood towns right by the shore. Other tsunamis are huge. These waves can be 130 feet (40 m) above the normal level of the sea. They can crash onto land with the same force as a wall of concrete. They **submerge** people, animals, buildings, and farms underwater. They can carry boats, vehicles, and parts of buildings miles inland. Entire coastlines can be altered by a tsunami.

Measuring Disaster

Scientists are working on systems that will give people some warning when a tsunami occurs.

Most tsunamis are caused by **earthquakes** at the bottom of the ocean.

→ **Seismologists** use **seismometers** to record when and where earthquakes happen and how strong they are.

When a tsunami begins, there is a sudden change in **sea level**.

→ Scientists have **sensors** in the oceans that can detect a deep tsunami wave passing over them.

Tsunamis cause more damage on areas of flat land at the coast.

→ Scientists make computer models of coastal areas to see how far tsunamis would travel inland. They then know which people to **evacuate**.

Natural disasters have taken place since Earth was formed. People have many ways of deciding what the world's worst natural disasters have been, from the deadliest disaster to the costliest. This book includes some of the worst disasters in history.

TSUNAMIS IN ACTION

Tsunamis usually happen when an earthquake makes the ground shake at the bottom of the ocean. This moves millions of tons of seawater and creates a series of waves at the ocean's surface. These waves can become tsunamis.

Tsunami Forces

Earth's outer layer, or **crust**, is made up of giant plates of rock. These huge, rocky slabs fit together like a jigsaw puzzle. They are called **tectonic plates**. The plates are always moving slightly because they sit on a layer of hot, melted rock deep inside Earth.

As the plates move, they push and slide against each other. When one sticks and then suddenly slips down, seawater rushes in to fill the gap. This sudden movement in the ocean causes giant waves, or tsunamis. These tsunamis travel quickly over long distances through deep water. As they near land, the waves slow down and pile up. They can build to great heights by the time they reach the shore.

Tsunami waves wash boats inland. They can crash into people and homes as they are tossed ashore.

6

Other Tsunamis

Some tsunamis happen when an underwater **volcano** explodes. Volcanoes shoot out hot liquid rock from beneath the crust when they erupt. They dislodge rocks around them and can cause large movements in the water. This can start tsunamis.

Other tsunamis happen when **landslides** send large amounts of rock or ice down into the water. In 1958, in Lituya Bay, Alaska, a landslide sent 90 million tons (81.6 million mt) of rock crashing into the bay. The result was a tsunami that reached 1,720 feet (525 m) up the slope on the other side of the bay.

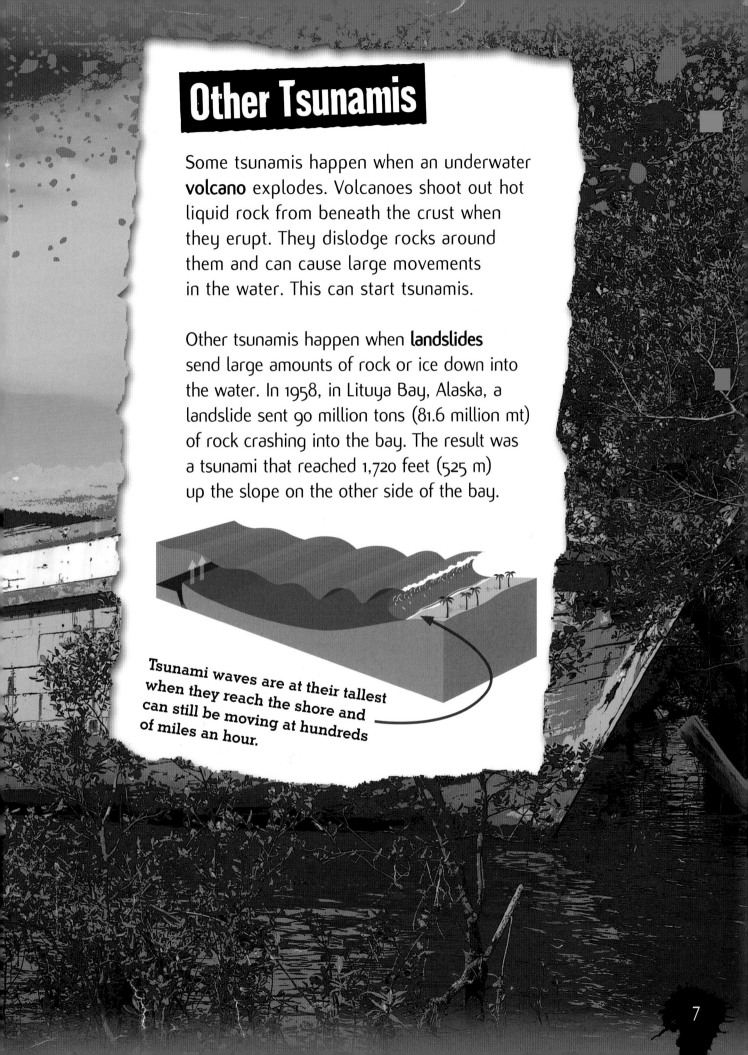

Tsunami waves are at their tallest when they reach the shore and can still be moving at hundreds of miles an hour.

10 FLORES SEA

A large earthquake occurred just off the north coast of Flores Island, Indonesia, early in the morning of December 12, 1992. It set off a series of devastating tsunamis, which arrived on the shores of Flores within 5 minutes.

Flores Sea

A Lost Island

Babi Island is a cone-shaped volcanic island that lay between Flores Island and the earthquake **epicenter**. The tsunami hit a narrow stretch of flat land on which two villages were located. The wave rose 23 feet (7 m) above sea level. It swept away all of the wooden homes on the island and killed 262 people. A few survivors managed to swim the 3 miles (5 km) to Flores Island, where they told gruesome stories of bodies left dangling in trees after the disaster.

On the Record

The tsunami carried water almost 1,000 feet (300 m) inland. Wave heights of over 80 feet (25 m) were reported on Flores Island.

The death toll from both the earthquake and tsunami was more than 2,000. The tsunami caused about half of those deaths.

The tsunami flattened trees and approximately 18,000 houses along the coast.

Only two people in the village of Nebe on Flores Island were killed. This is because the dense palm tree forest in front of their homes protected them.

A long, heavily populated **peninsula** off Flores was flooded by water that destroyed 80 percent of the area's wooden houses and killed 87 people.

9 CHILE

The tsunami that hit Chile on May 22, 1960, was caused by the largest earthquake recorded in the twentieth century. The earthquake itself was massive, but most of the injuries and deaths were caused by the tsunami that followed it, just 15 minutes later.

Far-Reaching Waves

The tsunami waves rose up to 80 feet (25 m) high on parts of the Chilean coastline. They wiped out entire areas and carried the remains of people's homes as far as 2 miles (3.2 km) inland. At least 200 people died in Chile alone. The shifts in the ocean floor caused by the quake were so enormous that the tsunami was powerful enough to reach as far as Hawaii and Japan, thousands of miles away, where they caused more destruction.

Chile

Tsunami waves traveled 6,200 miles (10,000 km) and hit Hawaii nearly 15 hours after the earthquake.

In Hawaii, 35-foot-high (11 m) waves caused millions of dollars of damage in Hilo Bay, killing 61 people.

When the waves reached Japan, 22 hours after the quake, the waves were still 18 feet (5.5 m) high.

In Japan, the tsunami was still strong enough to cause terrible damage and smash these ships into a bridge.

In Japan, the tsunami destroyed 1,600 homes and killed nearly 200 people.

Waves that approached California on the Pacific Coast of the United States were up to 5.6 feet (1.7 m) high. They damaged boats and **docks** in Los Angeles, San Diego, and Long Beach.

8 NANKAIDŌ

In 1946, the largest earthquake ever recorded in Japan shook the ground off the coast of Honshu, Japan's main island. It was a massive 8.1 magnitude quake and caused three major tsunamis. They inflicted terrible damage to the people and homes along the coast of Nankaidō district in southwest Japan.

Nankaidō

Striking the Coast

Japan experiences about 1,500 earthquakes every year, mostly small, because it sits above a total of four tectonic plates. The enormous Nankaidō quake struck on the evening of December 20. It shook most of Japan, from the largest central island, Honshu, down to Kyushu, destroying many homes and injuring many people. The worst loss of life happened within an hour when the tsunamis hit the coast.

On the Record

Of the three tsunamis, which struck 20 minutes after each other, the middle one was highest, with waves of up to 20 feet (6 m).

Japan was in turmoil in 1946, just after the end of World War II (1939–1945). It had heavy bomb damage, widespread hunger, and homelessness. The tsunami and earthquake made a bad situation worse.

Even before the earthquake, many people were homeless, such as these men sleeping on the steps of a Tokyo subway station.

The tsunamis completely washed away over 2,000 homes and destroyed tens of thousands more.

The worst damage happened on the Kii Peninsula, which was the land closest to the offshore epicenter.

About 1,362 people were killed by the tsunamis.

TOKYO-YOKOHAMA

Japan is hit by a tsunami at least once a year. The tsunami that occurred at noon on September 1, 1923, was set off by a huge undersea earthquake 60 miles (96 km) south of Tokyo, Japan's capital city.

Tokyo-Yokohama

A Day of Terror

The earthquake shook for more than 4 minutes. It caused tectonic plates around Sagami Bay to lift up by 6 feet (2 m) and to move horizontally by up to 15 feet (4.5 m). This rupture of the ocean floor generated a tsunami that reached heights of over 20 feet (6 m). It flooded many low-lying areas along the coast. The quake, tsunami and the subsequent fires and landslides they caused destroyed much of Tokyo and nearby Yokohama.

On the Record

A series of huge waves swept away thousands of people in Yokohama, the biggest port city in Japan.

The tsunami washed away dozens of villages.

The tsunami waves reached heights of 40 feet (12 m) at Atami, on the Sagami **Gulf**, destroying 155 homes and killing 60 people.

Each year, on September 1, there is a national Disaster Prevention Day in Japan.

The earthquake, tsunami, fires, and landslides killed about 140,000 people in total.

6 PAPUA NEW GUINEA

When a major earthquake struck off the coast of Papua New Guinea on July 17, 1998, it created one of the most destructive tsunamis to strike the country. Three large tsunami waves battered the region within minutes of the quake.

Papua New Guinea

Chaos

The epicenter of the quake was only 12 miles (19 km) off the coast of Papua New Guinea. When the tsunami waves hit the quiet fishing villages along a 19-mile (30 km) stretch of beach west of the town of Aitape, it was early evening and dark, causing chaos. Most people were in their homes and had been given no warning the quake and tsunami might happen. The tsunami killed over 2,000 people and left many more homeless.

On the Record

The largest of the tsunami waves were 30 feet (10 m) high.

Most of the deaths occurred in two villages on a narrow **spit** of land that separates the Sissano **Lagoon** from the ocean. Each had about 1,800–2,000 inhabitants. All of their homes were completely swept away.

The tsunami ripped palm and coconut trees out of the ground completely.

This school building was carried 213 feet (65 m) by the tsunami until it was caught in palm trees.

Paul Saroya, a survivor who lost eight members of his family, commented: "We just saw the sea rise up and it came toward the village and we had to run for our lives."

After the first three giant waves, there was a short rest before a final, less powerful wave hit. Within 20 minutes of the quake, the ocean was quiet again.

5 SANRIKU

A powerful earthquake occurred on March 2, 1933, in the Sanriku region of Japan. It generated a destructive tsunami that caused extensive damage along the coast.

Sanriku

Mighty Waves

The earthquake had a magnitude of 8.4 but it did little damage to buildings along the coast. Most of the damage was caused by the tsunami. This is because the earthquake occurred about 180 miles (290 km) off the coast of Japan. The shaking of the ground was less severe by the time it reached dry land. The large tsunami hit the coast 30 minutes after the quake. More than 3,000 people lost their lives in these devastating waves.

On the Record

About 5,000 houses in Japan were destroyed, of which nearly 3,000 were washed away.

At Ryori Bay, Honshu, waves 94 feet (29 m) high led to many deaths and terrible damage to homes and other buildings.

This is the area hit by the tsunami in 1933.

At the town of Taro, the waves reached a height of 33 feet (10 m), destroying 98 percent of the homes and killing almost half of its inhabitants.

The tsunami also caused slight damage in Hawaii, thousands of miles away, where a 9.5-foot (2.9 m) wave was recorded on the coast of the main island.

4 ANDAMAN SEA

Most of the earthquakes that happen in the Andaman Sea, even the larger magnitude earthquakes, do not usually cause big tsunamis. The earthquake that struck near the Andaman and Nicobar Islands of India, on June 26, 1941, was one of the biggest exceptions to this rule.

Andaman Sea

Tsunami Destruction

This major earthquake happened just before noon around 13 miles (20 km) west of Middle Andaman Island. The jolt in the seafloor caused a tsunami in the Andaman Sea and the Bay of Bengal. The wave hit India's east coast and Sri Lanka. It killed about 5,000 people on the hundreds of islands making up the Andaman and Nicobar Islands and along the east coast of India.

On the Record

The earthquake struck with a magnitude of 8.1. It caused buildings to shake in Chennai, in India, over 800 miles (1,300 km) away.

Some newspaper accounts from the time suggest that the tsunami may have been more than 4 feet (1.25 m) high. This would have submerged many low-lying parts of the region.

The low-lying Andaman and Nicobar Islands are the peaks of a submerged mountain range and are at high risk of being flooded by tsunamis.

The Moken people, a tribe of **sea nomads** in the area, have legends about the sea being sucked away before giant waves come. It is possible that some may have escaped to higher ground as soon as they saw the sea retreat.

The earthquake was caused by northward movement of part of Earth's crust. This same movement formed the Himalayan Mountains and the tallest mountain in the world, Everest.

3 MORO GULF

The Moro Gulf is the largest gulf in the Philippines. It is located off the coast of Mindanao Island, and is part of the Celebes Sea. On August 17, 1976, a powerful earthquake occurred in Mindanao and generated a tsunami that devastated the coastline along the Moro Gulf.

Moro Gulf

Midnight Killer

The earthquake struck a few minutes after midnight, when most people were asleep in bed. They had no idea what was about to hit them. Less than 5 minutes after the earthquake, huge tsunami waves reached the shore and swept through villages along the Moro Gulf, affecting 435 miles (700 km) of coastline. Official counts put the death toll for the earthquake and tsunami at more than 8,000, including those missing and never found. It is believed that the tsunami was responsible for 85 percent of those deaths.

On the Record

The 1976 tsunami was the most destructive ever to hit the Philippines.

Some of the tsunami waves reached heights of up to 30 feet (9 m).

The tsunami left over 90,000 people homeless.

Tsunami damage was widespread at Lebak on Mindanao Island in the Moro Gulf.

In some places, the tsunami waves roared 1,640 feet (500 m) inland, washing away hundreds of homes.

Eyewitnesses said the tsunami made houses rock like boats caught in a storm and sounded like the rumbling of many trucks together.

2 TŌHOKU

At 2:46 p.m. on March 11, 2011, a powerful undersea earthquake off the northeastern coast of Japan caused widespread damage on land. It also created a series of large tsunami waves. The waves devastated many coastal areas, especially in the Tōhoku region, and caused a major accident at a nuclear power station along the coast.

Tōhoku

A Powerful Tsunami

As well as hitting the coast of Japan, tsunami waves moved at speeds of up to 500 miles (800 km) per hour in the opposite direction. They swept up to 12 feet (3.6 m) high along the coasts of two islands in Hawaii and caused waves 5 feet (1.5 m) high along one of the Aleutian Islands, 2,455 miles (3,950 km) away. Hours later, tsunami waves were still 9 feet (2.7 m) high when they struck the coast of the United States.

On the Record

Most of the 19,300 deaths were caused by the tsunami waves.

One wave measured 33 feet (10 m) high and another swept 6 miles (10 km) inland.

The tsunami flooded many farms, towns, and villages along the coast, washing houses, boats, cars, trucks, and other **debris** along with it.

As the water from the tsunami washed back into the sea, it carried people and huge amounts of debris with it. Large stretches of land were also left underwater.

Tsunami waves wrecked the Fukushima nuclear plant. More than 60,000 people were evacuated from the surrounding area and high **radiation** levels mean that most have never been able to return home.

INDIAN OCEAN

On December 26, 2004, a huge undersea earthquake off the coast of the Indonesian island of Sumatra set off a devastating tsunami in the Indian Ocean. A series of massive waves caused widespread destruction in several countries around the ocean.

Indian Ocean

Worst Tsunami

The earthquake struck at 8:00 a.m. Within 2 hours, tsunami waves hit the eastern coasts of India and Sri Lanka, about 750 miles (1,200 km) away. Five hours after that, tsunami waves hit the coast of East Africa, more than 1,800 miles (3,000 km) away. The tsunami killed more than 225,000 people in 12 countries, with Indonesia, Sri Lanka, India, the Maldives, and Thailand suffering the worst damage.

On the Record

People were swept away in the waters, which arrived with little warning.

In the open ocean, the tsunami was less than 3 feet (1 m) high. When it reached the shores, its height increased to 50 feet (15 m) in some places.

The tsunami traveled at up to 500 miles (800 km) per hour.

Aceh, in Indonesia, was devastated by the tsunami in 2004.

The tsunami destroyed so many houses that 2 million people were made homeless.

Since the disaster, the countries surrounding the Indian Ocean have set up a joint early-warning system.

A survivor described being caught in the tsunami water full of debris as, "like being in a giant washing machine full of nails on a spin cycle."

WHERE IN THE WORLD?

This map shows the locations of the tsunamis featured in this book.

ATLANTIC OCEAN

Read the case studies about the tsunami in the Indian Ocean in 2004, the number 1 tsunami in this book, and the tsunami in Indonesia in 1992, which is number 10. How are they similar and how do they differ?

Describe in your own words some of the ways in which people can monitor tsunamis and give people enough warning to escape.

PACIFIC OCEAN

 Chile

What do you notice about the locations of these tsunamis? What does this tell you about the regions where tsunamis happen?

Sanriku

Tōhoku

Nankaidō

Tokyo-Yokohama

Andaman Sea

Moro Gulf

PACIFIC OCEAN

Indian Ocean

Papua New Guinea

Flores Sea

INDIAN OCEAN

GLOSSARY

crust Earth's outer layer of solid rock.

debris Loose waste material.

docks Partly enclosed areas in ports where boats load and unload.

earthquakes Sudden violent shaking of the ground.

epicenter Point on Earth's surface above the place where an earthquake started.

evacuate Get away from an area that is dangerous to somewhere that is safe.

gulf A deep inlet of the ocean or sea, almost surrounded by land, with a narrow entrance.

lagoon A stretch of salt water separated from the ocean or sea by a low sandbank or coral reef.

landslides Collapses of masses of earth or rock from mountains or cliffs.

magnitude Size, particularly of an earthquake, where 1 is small and 10 is the biggest.

peninsula A finger of land projecting out into a body of water.

radiation A type of strong, dangerous energy produced by nuclear reactions.

sea level The average height of the ocean's surface.

sea nomads People who live mainly in boats and move from place to place.

seismologists Scientists who study earthquakes.

seismometers Machines that measure the movement of the ground during a volcano or earthquake.

sensors Devices that detect and measure something such as wave height.

spit A narrow coastal land formation that is linked to the coast at one end.

submerge Completely cover with water.

tectonic plates The giant pieces of rock that fit together like a jigsaw puzzle to form Earth's crust.

tide The regular rise or fall of the ocean water at the coast.

volcano An opening in Earth's crust from which melted rock and hot gases erupt, often forming a cone-shaped mountain.

FURTHER READING

Books

Bailer, Darice. *Indian Ocean Tsunami Survival Stories* (Natural Disaster True Survival Stories). North Mankato, MN: Child's World, 2016.

Katirgis, Jane. *Scary Tsunamis* (Earth's Natural Disasters). New York, NY: Enslow Publishing, 2015.

Larson, Kirsten. *Tsunamis* (Devastating Disasters). Vero Beach, FL: Rourke Educational Media, 2015.

Websites

Due to the changing nature of Internet links, PowerKids Press has developed an online list of websites related to the subject of this book. This site is updated regularly. Please use this link to access the list: **www.powerkidslinks.com/nud/tsunamis**

INDEX